I Am an Inventor

Written by Mary-Anne Creasy

Flying Start
to Literacy®

Contents

Introduction

This is Don Morgan.
Don is a teacher
and a scientist, and he
is also an inventor.
He has invented an
amazing new
bike helmet.

This is the story about
how Don became
an inventor and the
steps that he followed
to get there.

$$\rightarrow \Delta p = mv - mu$$
$$\rightarrow \Delta p = m(v - u)$$
$$\rightarrow \Delta p = m \Delta v$$
$$Ft = m(v - u)$$
$$Ft = m \Delta v \quad \left\{ \begin{array}{l} \text{Impulse} \\ \text{Impulse} \end{array} \right.$$

new Inventors

...VENTORS 2007 EPISODE WINNER

Chapter 1
Don sees a problem

Twenty years ago, Don worked on a research project at a university. He was researching what happened to bicycle helmets when riders crashed.

Don set up experiments in his laboratory to test more than 100 different types of helmets.

Don also visited crash sites to see what happened to helmets when people crashed. It was part of his job to take the helmets back to the laboratory to study them.

Becoming an inventor

Step 1: Find a problem that needs to be solved.

During the experiments, Don found out that the helmets did not protect the riders' heads as well as they could. The lining inside the helmets was too hard. The lining needed to be much softer to protect a rider's head from the force of a crash.

Don knew that helmets needed to be safer, but no one was interested in what Don had found out from his experiments.

When Don's daughter was learning to ride a bike, he checked his daughter's helmet. He knew it was not as safe as it could be.

It was then that Don decided that he would have to make a safer helmet himself. He would become an inventor.

Chapter 2
A great idea

Don knew that the lining inside a helmet was the most important part of the helmet. He tried different ways to make the lining inside the helmet softer.

One day Don was at home preparing for one of his classes at the university when a great idea popped into his head.

He thought about using little foam cones inside the lining of a bicycle helmet. He thought that the foam cones would protect the rider's head from the crash.

Becoming an inventor

(Step 1) • • **Step 2:** Think of an invention that will solve the problem.

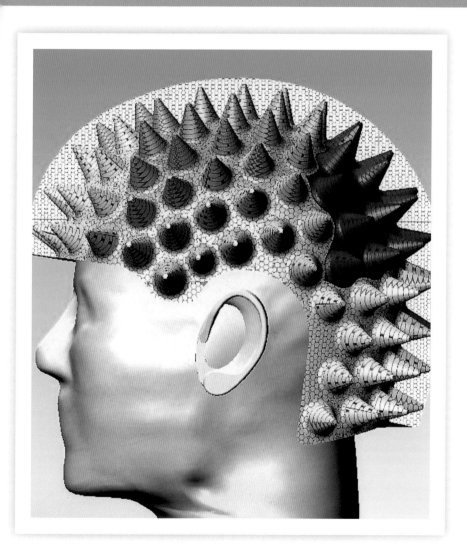

Chapter 3
Getting it down on paper

Don drew some pictures to see how the cones might work. Don thought that the cone was a good shape because a cone is strong and hard to crush.

He worked out that there must be soft cones next to the rider's head. He decided that the soft cones needed to be covered with foam that was harder than the cones but was not too hard. The harder foam made the helmet stronger.

Becoming an inventor

Step 1 • Step 2 • **Step 3**: Draw how your invention might look.

Hard outside shell of helmet

Lining layer

Layer of soft foam cones

Hard foam layer

Chapter 4
Don tests his idea

Don tested his new idea.

He built a hard metal head shape that had soft foam cones inside it. In his laboratory, Don used a machine to crash the helmet onto a hard surface to test what would happen in a bike crash.

The tests showed that the soft foam cones inside the helmet would protect a rider's head better than hard lining.

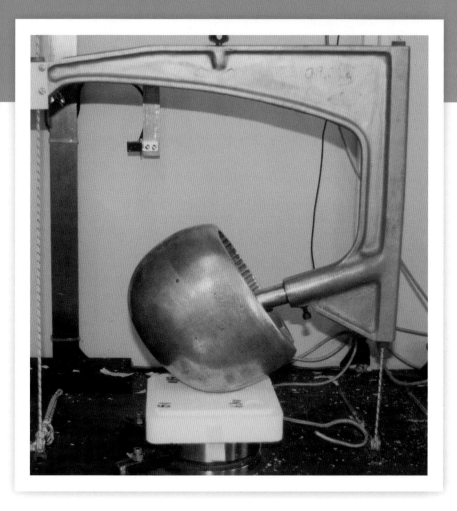

Becoming an inventor

Step 4: Test your idea to find out if it works.

Don knew his helmet would be much safer than other helmets. In a crash, it would protect the person wearing it better than other sorts of helmets.

Now Don needed to get his invention made.

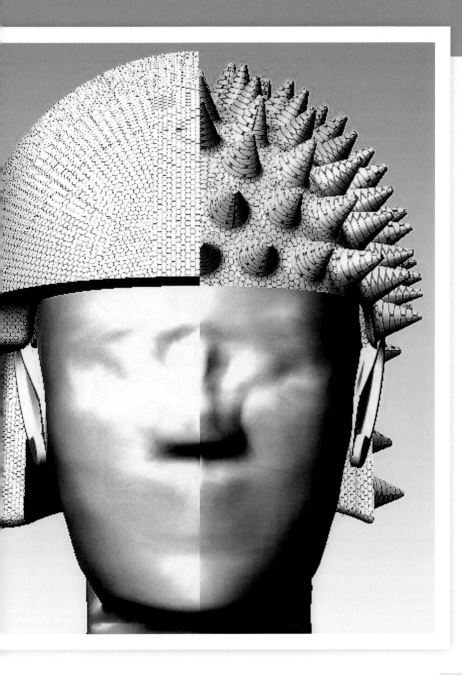

Chapter 5
Making the helmet

Don needed money to get his helmet made. He wrote many letters to people who made bicycle helmets, asking for their support, but he could not get anybody interested in his idea.

Step 1 •• Step 2 •• Step 3 •• Step

Becoming an inventor

Step 5: When you are sure that your invention works, get it made.

After many years of trying to get support for his idea, Don was ready to give up.

Don's family encouraged him to keep going. Eventually, Don was given the money he needed to get his helmet made.

When the helmet was eventually made, it was tested many times in a laboratory to make sure that it was safe for people to use.

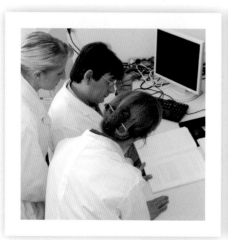

Chapter 6
Telling the world

Don was chosen to go on a television show called *The New Inventors* to demonstrate his invention. He showed how his helmet was made and why it was safer than other helmets.

Out of 120 inventions demonstrated that year, Don's invention was chosen as the best. Don was named the Inventor of the Year.

Don's helmets will now be made and sold in many parts of the world.

Step 1 • • Step 2 • • Step 3 • • Step 4

Becoming an inventor

Step 5 •

Step 6: Advertise your invention so that people know about it.

Conclusion

Don's story shows how being an inventor takes a lot of imagination, a lot of time and a lot of effort.